Ex

Th

CW01642014

Excerpts from *The Scenic World* by Matthew Gregory

First published by If a Leaf Falls Press
London, 2025

ISBN: 9781068741111
First printing

Cover by Alice Ray: alice-ray.com

Designed and typeset by O. Tong in
Sorts Mill Goudy and IM Fell French Canon

Printed and bound by TJ Books

This publication is kindly sponsored by Daniel Handler

Excerpts from *The Scenic World*

Matthew Gregory

If a Leaf Falls Press 2025

Contents

I

II

III

Excerpts from *The Scenic World*

I

A Room in Paris, 1855

An alchemist's gas lamp
reaches shakily into one corner,
some paintings nobody
has a particular opinion on
are nailed over
rose ballroom wallpaper.

And on the long bed
the middle-aged poet,
Gérard de Nerval.

He would appear restful
if it wasn't for his eyebrows meeting
like two dark horses
in the middle of his forehead.
He is dreaming of the beautiful apple
he palmed only a few days before
on Ile Saint Louis
and the grief of a wormhole
in the thing perfected.

He wakes all of a sudden.
He takes his collection
Les Chimères
down from its cramped shelf
and cuts it in half at the spine
with a knife.
He will clean
every sentence

A Room at the Grand Hotel des Roches Noires, 1971

Madame likes to air the double she takes for eight weeks
on the sea-facing east wing.

She has written twelve postcards to Brussels in a month.

Her tone—*La mer est jolie*—is light and blasé though
she counts six instances of the word
                                        ténèbres.

Arthritis has touched her best hand. Outside the sea
glances her way with distance

where once everything in the world was a man
asking her to dance.

On one shelf in ribbons, her empty hatbox deepens

into deeper hatboxes that collapse slowly
                    into the green pinochle halls
                    of the pinochle men she knew.

Madame dreams in the window chair

and sees her postcards
from the Roches Noires
fly lightly down
                    over the swathe of sea
                    from the undercarriage
                    of an albatross.

The ocean bird migrating   but so everything seems
at this point

the cad with a tall white grin
throwing double sixes at midnight
fresh oysters with their slight cologne
in the backseats of young France

The concierge is calling her
—*Madame. Madame?*

An old albatross the scuffed white of lobby magazines.

An old albatross, but content as she wanders off the edge
of the continent.

A Room on the Capitaine Paul-Lemerle, 1941

Yesterday a deckhand confused the new land
with a cloudbank and its own flocks and shepherds
and white houses in the cloud's country.

The sea is green at night
                                        a violent blue by day
and wider and deeper than the dreams of André Breton.
André Breton is aboard the *Capitaine*.

He is writing to someone, 1am. His bunk wobbles
in the rough passage and his gaslamp swings.
On his wrists the eczema has come up again.

His yellow sleeve is spotted with ink as he spills
his hand across the page. He is writing to his wife
or to Nadja but won't decide who until he signs off.

He is describing the luminescence that rises
through the ocean at night and follows the *Capitaine*.

First there is only a pulse, the propeller turning
up green sparks, stirring them with its long ladles
before the lighted halls of plankton appear.

It follows us, Dearest, disappearing for days
then returning in waves like the mind to a place.

In every light shoal he sees something he remembers.

In every hall an empty lectern and shipment papers.

André Breton walks a Sorbonne in his head
and goes from room to room, to look for the lights
left flickering.

He writes how the crew saw
a manta rise in the glow
with its dark studies under one arm of its cloak,
circle once then wing slowly out of their surveillance.

A Room in the Pacific Palisades, 1979

well here's something I never did like Tolstoy awful much
dontcha know Betty Beverly hell I mean Brenda
the old novelist was saying as he thumped the tablecloth
just missing the silver goblets and service plates
steaming in drifts before him.
                                        Bald and small he sat
across from the young actress he wrote to habitually
praising in his endless beautiful trains
and clauses that led often now
                                        to great tiredness.
Against the one amber lampshade they were profiled
a grey king and confidante. Where the sitting room dimmed
at the periphery, characters from his years abroad stepped
out of dark friezes and spoke—
                                        a lush with remarkable tattoos
needled like varicose, an ancient 'legionnaire', the beautiful boy
leading a wolfhound by the reins, and young Jean Genet who
no, no, he'd not met Jean Genet.
                                        On Montmartre he'd loved
so many whores. In the young actress opposite
he sometimes saw them play across her features:
an eyebrow arched back fifty years, the nose upturned
or lengthened in the dark, a mole drew itself on her cheek.

Thérèse, Sylvie, or Margot, was it, who sat with him now
with the fifty, one hundred, one thousand
who seemed to be there, leaning on an elbow, listening
brightly, always just across from him, in the other chair.

A Room in Taiwan, 2010

And how many desert miles of the web
has she crossed tonight searching
for the home address of Mastroianni.

Mastroianni is no longer among us.
She doesn't know this so continues
her drift from one ruined domain

to the next one, signing herself in
to empty guestbooks as she goes.
I would like to write to Mr Marcello Mastroianni

please if anyone know where he is.
I dream us in light of stars and great city Rome.
I want to be like kiss of Anita Ekberg.

Mastroianni whose thousand pictures
in these forums lose him on pages
like palimpsests of man on top of man

where this girl, at her tropical desk,
who lists for his deep, romantic heart
touches a hit-counter, once, in the dark.

A Room in Naples, 2005

Lo Spagnolo, unshaven, up in bed
on his last morning as a free man.

Sunlight grids his face on one side
as it enters through the shutters.

An early sea-mist lifts from the hits
his boys left at angles in an alley.

Heavy now, at forty, the bite gone
somewhat from his muscles,

all of his superstitious tattoos unravel
to a quiet place in the country.

At this age he's just started reading—
there's the unlikely Leopardi

some Monica or Mona gave him
for St Valentines. He tries 'Silvia'

though puts it aside when he reaches
'*...where my life was burning out*'.

Isabella, beside him, puts out a thigh
with its unfinishable sentence.

He swallows his salve from the poet.
Son of a bitch. Why do they do that.

A Room at the Sasquatch Symposium, Montana, 1993

Raymond L. Wallace keeps his shtum.
Feels sadder than he has for ages.
1967 and his monkey suit shambling
out of focus and into the hungry tract
    of the American imagination.

A Room in Platinum, 1994

thinking how simian he was
the singer
ate waffles and sat
in his observatory at dawn

watching the willows
come round like longhairs
in the mist

but he felt cold among them
and fudged the television on
to himself sleepwalking
part of the tour
inchoate somehow but there
how various to see himself

nobody would enter the house
he might not leave his couch again
the singer using
one room out of fifteen

sat on the floor of the whale
like Jonah and stirred
his pot of beans

A Room at the Oregon Coast Aquarium, 1992

the young keepers come   with their steadies to smoke
  in the white recesses   of the observation bay
for a long moment   nothing   then the tiniest fraction
of him slivers the surface   his dorsal melted over
  those beautiful clouds   patched around his eyes
woah   the girls are lost   in him the first time
he breaches out   turns whiteside   then spews
  a beachball   some metres   above the tank
they'll watch   a while longer   then he's alone
until morning   a teenage whale   listening   to the deep
  convolutions   sounding   inside his head
the intimate sea   mixed up with   human ordinance
Keiko at the glass   his dark eye on   the dome complex
  in the starlight   empty except   many strange forms
of life   the whale   on his back   gazing up
at the horse   the scorpion   the implements
  certain other   mythic shapes   more his size
he relaxes his flippers   he will fall backwards
into the sky

A Room in Pëtkwo

An observatory for the antics of remote weather.
Waterspouts and cyclones spinning up
on the furthest oceans. And an eye
watching over it all. The blurring vanes
of the anemometers high on the dome,
the dome, its curvilinear sides and funnels,
the fins and aerials, of an inoperative flying machine.
The century, here, an inoperative machine.
And the man who is charged with all this
watches dials and oscillating nibs
tighten their circles to the mad dense scream
of something enormous coming
into consciousness and moving on the sea.
It is impressive. You can impress someone
telling them you're guardian of the weather—
like the only personable woman in this town.
Often on the flimsy pier, pale Miss Zwida
in her straw hat, drawing beautifully
the faint taxonomies of seashells.
Shells in their complicated frequencies.
Or one time—a long line of hotel palms
leaning into wind like a stranded company
of islanders, ready to leave Pëtkwo
for time far away. But this was rare.
The day before, he surprised Miss Zwida
on her wicker chair, as a new front
darkened its interest a few leagues out.
Pointing to where the registers scribbled
continuously under the observatory dome

he said *it's like receiving a secret letter*
from one of the world's great authors
but late, into the night, you realize how
cold and far from us his brilliance has come.

A Room in Florence, 1266

More of a dog extended in all directions
over the thin rug, in the stone-wall cloister
the man begins to kick and whimper
while his gut, in good voice, escapes his belt.

The sleeping face is moist and flavourful
intensified by the little bursts of lightning
in purples across his cheeks and nose.
Mist. Then a kind of softish light. Certain tropes

of lyric poems pass into the scene where
the friar, this Loderingo, snores in deep chords
triumphantly out for all his sermons
and petitions. Marshes beyond the city walls

thicken with lowlife and schismatic
but the friar is dreaming, vague transactions
and soft flatteries, on an ideal balcony.
He has toothache in one molar but his dream

fills the space where the throb should be
with a pale horse, clip-clopping on cobbles.
His head is full of hoofbeats as the horse trots
through Florence without a rider or cause.

A Room in the Crystal Palace, New Year's Eve, 1853

"...inside Iguanodon a select party
dine on turbot and mock turtle
till cognac and the humours
send them, hats in hand, to bed
tiny formal spectres of men
moving across the crescent lawns
of the starlit palace grounds
the sculptor, a Mr Benjamin Watkins
alone at last, nurses his head
in his hands before it can fall
forwards like a glass of water
into wild surmises of the hour
then steps from the hollow cast
scene of 'a most unmatchable dinner'
down from the rutted girth
to look his model in the eye
the eye chipped into the skull
the same whorl he'd grafted onto
Ichthyosaurus and Megalosaurus
but dull recognition then
the gaze less a giant reptile's
gaze than the bulbous fixéd
one of his creationist friend
the venerable Sir Richard Owen..."

A Room in the Republic, (Capua), 73BC

[FRAGMENT]

it's forty degrees when the sun really means it
moving light columns
through the dark ludus

overhead the white villa is empty

the menials, culinarians, gone
leaving

walls glancing with lizards
a few mountain acanthus
petrified in their pots

the house treasures
looted or shattered through the corridors

morning after morning from the low foothills
daylight

a madness returning to a mind
barely restored

~~*nihil semper restituitur*~~

nothing will ever be restored

inside the complex barefoot, living on

last pomegranates and dust

domina watches petals blow through the baths

II

A Portrait of Matteo Lonardi

I'm with Matteo at café Gambrinus,
in Piazza Plebescito, Napoli.
He is in love with Palma Bucarelli,
the granddaughter of the critic, Palma Bucarelli.

It might be my favourite place in the whole of Italy.
The rooms are a curtained opal green
with swannecked interiors multiplying
in enormous mirrors to infinity.

It is a little too much, though, for Matteo.
It is better to not overstate.
It is better to wear your cashmere
as if a horse had rolled on it.

Divino, was what his uncle, the Visconte
would say to literally anything.
Matteo had seen a unicorn.
O *divino*.

His lineage ran through
the bloodblack drawing-rooms
of the Italian alps, France and Germany.
It went innocently.

It ran with the Piedmontese
in bayonet charges that flowed
over foothills in the two horns
of the mountain chamois.

It commanded the first musket shot that went screaming
through the air
like the deathscared bleat
of the mountain chamois, skittering across the parquet
in the Visconte's lodge.

It went innocently.
Sometimes it became tan and conversational
and grew into a boy
like Matteo Lonardi.

Two cream-filled cornettos arrive on a napkin.
It is as if someone has lopped the horns
from a mountain chamois.
We eat messily.

Palma has not responded to any of his messages.
She snows blondly across his phone
in a white cornfield, in the photo
he took in Tuscany, at the Casa Bucarelli.

Matteo is reading *The Great Gatsby.*
It is so-so, he tells me.
Of course Gatsby wasn't quite the real thing,
he was only an American.

He knocks on the spiral darkling veneer
of our corner table at Gambrinus.
A truly rich and beautiful country.
You should see that place.

Circumvesuviana

In the old paintings, the volcano
sits for its portrait heavy-browed
and insists it will smoke
a thin, white cigarillo.

I'm watching little pink and white clouds
campaign across Vesuvio,
paused meaningfully for now—
the flanks a vitriolic green.

In the back of this pasticceria
a boy is offering his arms
in desperate figures to explain
his whereabouts last night.

His girlfriend is silent.
The gelato counter hums in the heat.
The frothing percolator
reaches its crisis point.

In the cramped ancient quarters
this scene a hundred times,
a thousand times.
Vesuvio has seen Roman, late-Roman

and neo-Roman and heard
a girl quietly crying in a courtyard
deranged with statuary
and nightflowering orange.

Vesuvio erupts in a cyclical way.
A herd of scooters.
The prefect and his papyrus.
Girl capturing a tear.

Each one standing as they were touched
lightly across the face
by the anointing hand.
Each one to carbon.

C'è un detto.
There is a saying.
Che abbiamo a Napoli.
That we have in Naples.

Anyone who has stood a while
under its shadow
has felt themselves very far
from where they are.

In this courtyard, with clementines—
Girl capturing a tear, and another
and another.
But this particular one.

The Ambassadors

Halfway up the mountain there is a window
barely noticeable if it wasn't the only window
flaring in the late sun. The house is white,
preternaturally white, and the air around it also white.
I'm working in my room far below
the mountain in question. What I'm working on
might be better accomplished if I just walked
the spiral road up the mountain
through its atmosphere of fern, alpine crocus, moss
and knocked at the white door, to be invited in
by the mysterious embassy there—
who will appear first as a pale hand opening
the latch onto a corridor and more
of their company. My work would be finished.
No more of the headaches and tense missives
in my room under the mountain.
My hosts would lead me down a gentle flight
to the garden and my place at their table,
where I'd find myself surprisingly topical and agile
in the conversations of several
unknown eminences, who switch lightly between
past and present couriers, the character
of bergamot oranges, the wolverine's potency
while scenting carrion, a snowball planet
and somehow, one of my own recent poems.
I'd eat golden things, that once eaten
leave only the delicate shape of a flavour
with infinite connotations. Then much later
I would rest my head on the table

to listen to the densely patterned exchanges
of my new friends, sounding something
like many books being read by the wind
in a high place. My head on the table,
then my head in the lap of the benevolent sovereign
who will stroke my hair and recount to me
the dark passages and bright alcazars
of our history, until I fall asleep there
in his patter. But the hand would withdraw,
the front door never open, the spiral road roll
back down the mountain. So I will continue
to write letters to these white addresses.

Hans Castorp in the Mountains

Time stuns us with its leaps
and reversals
or envelops us inside
a huge, motionless clause.
Think of me as swimming
in my own clouded levels,
where the station clocks
of the Massif confound
the station clocks of Brussels.
I could give so many illustrations
of what happens to a mind
transported in this mountain air.
Between two blinks a dark valley
can be a whole polity
of sunlight, with golden steeples,
boulevards and streams
of folk there and then, not.
A lammergeyer overhead
is not ever a lammergeyer.
A hand of cards at bridge
can open like a blade
onto a bitter age.
The heartsick patients suffer
from a type of happiness.
From my balcony, I can see
the old-time skier of the lodge
pick his way up one
of the three colossal teeth
still blue with winter falls.

He is this afternoon's Rousseau.
So many skiers have climbed
for the clear white note
of a loneliness that is perfect
and every year
when the sun is a wild semaphore
a man will go up there
to find something
like a seam in the light
leaving his equipment
to the slopes, as if to say
Herr Scholl or Herr Klein
ascended to a certain height.

Palms at Anacapri

But the year widens and arrives at that point
when the sun makes its definitive statement,
burning those who doze off on balconies.
The billionaires' yachts network in the port.
The folding chair is called into requisition,
the boater and nylon blouse are harvested
from their long racks. All are agreed
that it is the time of coconut vendors
to bend spectra from their hoses, to splash
the Germans arriving, luminous and early, at the resort.
It is now that the first of the Milanese girls
roll into town in striped, billowing pants,
abstract strokes in pristine restaurants.
Clownfish play peekaboo in marble aquaria.
All this happens under the watch of the three
in the square outside Hotel Anacapri.
Long, tall, cool migrants waded in from elsewhere,
they stand like every tableau of ancient travellers—
sunbeat, heads down, stooped after their voyage
on one of the wild, historical seas.
The saddest tree. These three had an ancestor
somewhere in the violent Pacific
with the grey, reticulated body of a crocodile
gradually ending in a green spray.
The tallest thing for miles. At the end of everything—
this symbol of the infinite liminal
arrived at and departed, until the symbol
doesn't know whether it's coming or going.
The summer races on and we see

their dark bursts against aquatint and magenta,
the blonde American girl twirling her straw,
taking their measure. Quite soon
and without announcement there is a day
when the last beach towel remains where it fell
under a light rain. A song traces across
the lobby tiles and hotel porphyry—
...when Bostonians find themselves again
in Boston they wonder at Capri palms...
Then foam tufts the beach, the season closes.
The island is the last island, day and night chase
each other in a bewildering colour series,
the waves exhume turtles and human plastics,
the last things, bare and boned in this last
utterance of a fragmentary light:
the palm tree knows the world as tourist.

Apostrophe to Disrepair

Like a city you would think of sometimes
where everything slipped towards the equator
in a swoon brought on by so much sun,
where you might enjoy an afternoon drinking wine
unlicensed by anyone,
where a word might be spoken
without addenda hanging from it
like a nest of wires.
The leaning houses,
the leaning lines of red, yellow and white houses,
with porticoes irregular and surprising
as drawings of porticoes by an infant master.
A city, like an overexposed and faded photograph
but a city where anxiety
was a funny thing nobody understood
as they talked expansively about the way
the mind was similar to a company of breezes
or anchovies boiling out at sea or tufa warming
the world with its emanations.
A city, broken down like a soft old horse
knackered by ducal processions, then by revolutions,
by men pulling her to market, the great markets,
now giddy and silly and light
on her legs in a simple valley.

45. *Maradona in the Azteca*

A mustard-coloured car drags itself along the street
of a neighbourhood where spaces are oblong or square
then tails off into a blue garage where the engine
becomes asthmatic, kicks up, then peters out abruptly

and the man on the boiling leather waits to see if
his thoughts compose themselves after the kind of day
where thoughts are a group of white balloons
released loose and uncomprehending into the sky

and perhaps they do, because he steps out of the car
carefully with his yellow salesman's suit clean-pressed
and leaves the engine that carries him around
to head towards the bulge of white plum and magnolia

then down the little drive, to the bay window's edge
where inside, the television plays a slow Mexican wave
of businessmen and contrabandists and vendors
of Argentina who'll return later to circuits in the dust.

90. *Zidane in the Stade de France*

The young helper draws her troupe of school children
across the Champ de Mars, one sunburn after the other,
the trees and sky a stunning mix of crème de menthe,
and they reach the point where the Eiffel Tower is at its best

and the kids are awed for a moment, and then, not so much
as they return to fitful spans and fascinations,
whether their baseball caps peak up, sideways or back to front,
an oozing bag of eclairs, the weird bug in the grass

but one of the group, a boy in a faded t-shirt and shorts
trails behind his friends, to gaze alone at the Eiffel Tower
that in turn considers him, a quiet giant on long legs
about to stride across the Seine or reach an arm into heaven.

+30. Messi in the Camp Nou

The guy in the greasy t-shirt and his sunk-eyed girlfriend
sit in their little Ronda somewhere outside the city.
They've pulled up to watch storm clouds browse
the tops
of the sand-coloured apartment blocks and basilicas,
the scrub and dust bristling with electricity in the darkness.
The couple begin to fumble. The girl deals with his belt
with her long fingernails, and tosses it carefully
onto the backseat.
Somewhere an owl tunes into a mouse. The radio fizzes
in the dashboard with a shaky station from the capital,
where a loco commentator trips over his tongue
and ten thousand others lose their voices in the stadium.
Only the couple are listening as the dark cloud opens
and rolls like a limousine across Barcelona.
Static and announcements. There are bewildering figures.

Ecuador

Someone was walking evenly over the bronze sand
in a careful line to where the sea slopped
and churned in the large waste. I walked parallel
to my invisible company, never breaking up their prints,
coming to a standstill as the surf dragged its hissing
white sheet back downwards. Whoever
I was following had swum for it, out across
the cove, never looking back, to one of the great liners.
A slowly sliding estate of brilliance in the dark
reached at a backstroke, my invisible partner
was rescued by a light craft, sluiced into the landing bay
of the giant ship, then lifted onto the upper deck.
Towelled roughly and made to drink some measures
of a mercurial brandy, he was undressed, then dressed
by an anonymous suite of servants, who spoke
in the hot rain of a New World Spanish
he couldn't quite place. His first impressions
were of beneficence, light, and a promise
spanning its giant rooms around him
with a creak. A life here. But broader
than it'd been for years and filled with the murmur
of conspiratorial voices who'd relay
a warm, continuous line of currency and news
to his consciousness. He would be led at last
to a padded bunk, with its electric light, intercom
and a porthole's clouded eye onto the horizon—
and then? The morning skyline. And its blue frames
falling into each other infinitely, each one
a vacancy aflame with some possible life.

Somewhere, he could walk out onto another beach
and stop the first person he saw, a tiny boy
with miniature nose, ears and feet
as if blown from fine glass and breathed into being,
pedalling an enormous cane rickshaw
over the lonely stretch. Dumbly, he would hand him
the disintegrated file of his old life
with its few names, addresses and scars
for everything piled in the rickshaw.
Certain mornings people wash up here
with their wild heads like palm nuts
that've toured the ocean for years on the current
of a memory of some original departure.
The sun coming up on the sea with a blue cheer.
The rich, valueless flotsam littering the boy's cart.
Where are we? *¿Dónde estamos?* We are finally here.

Poste

He writes from the south. He writes between researching
and politely expiring.

He writes from behind a partition, from the hot sand,
from banded shadow.

He writes from the beach, on a collapsible sunchair for hours
among collapsible sunchairs.

He writes at 3pm, as focus on his assignment shifts to the waves
of locals backstroking.

He writes nothing for several days. He writes of the great lapse
in the Montgomery palms.

He writes from a Sorrento gelateria, of the shadowy associates
pictured with the proprietor.

He writes from a table at the Hotel Syrene. He writes at 8 o'clock.
He writes, of diverse *scampi*.

He writes from a porphyry foyer, from the hotel fountains'
crystal insignia.

He writes of a general postponement, empty trunks in a soft fall
of rain on the beach.

He writes how his thesis sprawls out like a peninsula town
in this reliquary heat.

He writes, ah, the great thesis, Europe, sad thesis...

III

Excerpts from *The Scenic World*

"It seemed just as if the typhoon were a part of his programme..."
JULES VERNE, *Around the World in Eighty Days*

"World's simpliest..."
NIKON

Page: 7

You may encounter lizards, such as this one.
He is easing into his veins by lying very still on a rock
in the popular town of Amalfi.
Notice the slant eyes continue even while
the body does not.
Lizards seem to agree on something
          with the rocks,
taking up to an hour to change their theme.
The humour of rock is perhaps subtle, and slow.

There are also people in Amalfi, as well as lizards.
Frequently the temperature
will climb in their heads
when the sun comes out.
They may throw bread or wine or sharp phonemes
          across tablecloths at each other.
They may move their hands much faster.
If we took the temperature of the lizards and the people
it would be about the same.

Page: 67

You may encounter an older language.
The word *metafora*
is the ghost of the word *metaphor*
for example.

This girl, Annamaria, is laughing at a silly *metafora*
a boy made up.
She is smiling quietly to herself
with her lips the colour of an expensive book.
The wit of her country is not
especially well received in the world today.
Though, she has the soft profile of a Roman
Belladonna.
This look was once extremely popular.

Page: 74

You may encounter flagstones, such as these in Naples.
They have remained grey, uncomplaining flagstones
for seven or eight centuries.
Each was chipped so that horses wouldn't forget their hooves
            on wet days
or so that when blood opted out of the busy life
            of the body
the horses could still maintain their footing.
It is difficult to comprehend the hours of blood and sun
these faces have witnessed.
The closest link we have to either is this
young woman dressed as a Lindt chocolate egg,
an ungraceful oval
of cardboard sections and crimson tinsel
in the month before Christmas.
Secretly her red expensive shoes are breaking
her morale.
Her anonymity as confection has men come to prolong
her demonstration,
though it is hard to blame them.
It is dully raining, and her hair is cinnamon and her eyes
               rainy abstractions
surprising here and there in the wet on the flagstones.
Her eyes are green. They were green. This is worth noting.

Page: 80

You may encounter scenery, such as in Vietri.
The Mediterranean is the same colour
as this girl's iris.
This could mean she has been gazing into the waves
her whole life
or for generations.

She is balancing on the volcanic tufa barefooted.
Where she is standing the coast could cut
her feet with its long jaw.
Her name is Federica.
She is learning English, gradually
but with beautiful purpose.
She is looking longingly at some backpackers looking
at her longingly.
The coin-op telescope and man consider each other.

Page: 105

You may encounter a rainstorm outside
while you are inside.
Such as in this resonant baroque arcade
of seraphim and grapes at 3.20pm.
Nowhere else in the world
could you achieve this perspective on rain
as it sends white bars through
the moving parts of the day outside.

Some of the droplets are landing
on the soft down of dying palm trees,
the blunted marble lions
or a litter of kittens curled
inside some old political headlines.
Some of the droplets are landing
on the haircut of a resilient midfielder
growing on the head of a boy.

Perhaps some droplets crash softly
onto the winged suspension
of Monica Bellucci's eyelashes
as she ducks into a slow cab in Milan.
It is something to imagine this rain
touching the follicles of famous women
though standing in your damp soles
rain washes each distinction
to something less than its beginning.

If you listen during rain you will hear
only the hiss of universal fame.
This sudden moustache flies past
on a scooter shouting *figlio di puttana*
at maybe you and the yellow clouds.

Page: 172

You may encounter a pigment in two different sources
such as in the eyes of this goldfish and this dalmatian.
It is a wistful or cumulus colour.
The dalmatian has its muzzle in the green fountain basin
and is taking water that may send parasites kicking into
    its bowels.
The goldfish submerged here since the Bourbon princes are slowly
    disintegrating,
many of them with clotted gills and their soft flanks
softer where time has touched them.
In many ancient beautiful parks there is a big sign that says
This water is not for drinking.
This green water is what Americans would call *European.*
The precise tincture of Bourbon princes remains unknown.

Page: 190

You may encounter a busted umbrella.
It has been raining
in Piazza Plebescito.
The rain has put a lot into this—
there are a number of busted umbrellas
with their stalks
snapped and watery petals open.

The umbrellas are flowers or something
opening their spokes
onto several contingencies.
Each leads back to the wet unclenched hand
of a man, or woman.
This one, for example,
her latest etching turned into a scroll
against the storm
as she stands feeling for a moment.
That idea you had about something, something
and umbrellas is entirely gone.

Page: 200

You may encounter an objective standard.
This young man, Giulio, for instance,
has not forgotten the slow methodology
of perfect espresso
his mother taught him with her hands.
He no longer has to measure or time
this operation—
the heat communes surely
in his brain
and he stirs a small, burnished spoon
into the set of cups his family keeps
and soon one tiny, explosive *caffè*
waits impatiently for you to enjoy it.
Things can really happen in this country.

Page: 235

You may encounter intolerance, as in this girl's of the French.
The French are unhygienic and their language a mouthful of feathers
the girl says, pointing her finger at something vaguely
ahead of her.

But this girl is extremely fond of her papa's cuisine.
If you were to disagree with his linguine or the way
he does steak Milanese you would soon understand something
of indefinite origin.

Page: 240

You may encounter a whale gone astray
such as this one, in the bay of Amalfi.
She has breached
not far from the bathers
who are surprised by something
so large this close to them.
When she blows she brings to mind
postcards of the famous volcano.
One of her flukes makes a melancholy signal
over the sea
and crashes down emphatically.
This only momentarily alters
the temperate waters and fine weather
and soon people can continue
with their *chiacchierata* and aftersun balms
on the improving gold of their bodies.
Aside from the greygreen of the whale
gold is predominant in Amalfi.

Page: 245

You may encounter a blue bee-eater
striking brilliantly
like the genius of blueness itself
through the Orto Botanico's
palm shadows.
On the other hand, you may not also.

Page: 272

You may encounter the sound of a wolf howling
in the small mountain town of Pogerola.
The sound is going from one side of rock to another.
At first it sounds like a mournful dog but then
there is a long note sharper and emptier
than a mournful dog.
It is as if the small ball thrown for you became suddenly
considerable in flight.
Wolves have flourished in the south of this country as things
deteriorate
in other areas, such as in waste-disposal, for example.
Several American tourists
have made sightings but were unable to recount the moment
digitally.
They are here for Herculaneum, vongoles, the ancient fort.
The wolf continues to howl, not quite believing it.

Page: 285

You may encounter what it was that moved a people
to build duomos and cornices and statuary
all over this country.

Watch this young man in the sit-down pasticceria
thoughtfully squeeze this cream
let each dream blossom in an immense space
on top of these rum babas and sfogliatelle
before achieving form.

Page: 300

You may encounter something in the narrow street
where you've walked many times already.
    A broken wall
risen out of the ground where there wasn't one before.
It belongs to no particular moment
in this peoples' architecture.
A sudden formation laid down in the interstices
    of the afternoon.

The street ends here and continues over the other side
where evening falls
on the cobbles and gutterwater and a riderless vespa
    shaking in fits by the curb.
Figures begin to drift from the doorways.
Here is the girl, Annamaria, who writes for the *Gazzetta*.
She appears in sharp boots and navy poloshirt
walking very quickly, in profile
through concentric circles of dusk.
Perhaps she is going to cover the mysterious wall
    for her newspaper.
But watch, as she somehow skirts around it
vanishing down the squeezed alleys and their systems
    of buckets winched
suddenly upwards to the higher floors.

Notes

A Room in Paris, 1855.
Gérard de Nerval, Symbolist poet who died on the banks of the river Seine, in the winter of 1855.

A Room in the Grand Hotel des Roches Noires, 1971.
The hotel was a glamorous hub for the gambling and sporting sets in the early part of the 20th century.

A Room on the Capitaine Paul-Lemerle, 1941.
The *Capitaine Paul-Lemerle* was a transatlantic vessel that smuggled a number of intellectuals and artists out of a Vichy-controlled France in the 1940s. Among them were André Breton and Claude Levi-Strauss.

A Room in the Pacific Palisades, 1979.
The writer is the novelist Henry Miller.

A Room in Taiwan, 2010.
Marcello Mastroianni, famous for his role in Fellini's *La Dolce Vita* and 8½.

A Room in Naples, 2005.
'Lo Spagnolo', Raffaele Amato, a Camorrista, arrested in 2005.

A Room at the Sasquatch Symposium, 1993.
Raymond L. Wallace, the Bigfoot hoaxer from Missouri.

A Room in Platinum, 1994.
The singer in the poem is Kurt Cobain, in the last year of his life.

A Room in the Oregon Coast Aquarium, 1992.
Keiko, the male orca who starred in the 1993 Warner Bros production, *Free Willy*. The whale, who had a bent dorsal fin, was released into the wild in 2002, after spending the majority of his life in captivity, but stranded himself a year later.

A Room in Pëtkwo.
Pëtkwo, a coastal town in Italo Calvino's novel, *If On a Winter's Night a Traveller*

A Room in Florence, 1266.
Loderingo degli Andalò, one of the profligate 'Jovial Friars', found among the hypocrites in the Eighth Circle of Dante's *Inferno.*

A Room in the Republic (Capua), 73 BC.
The ludus is that of Lentulus Batiatus, ill-fated dominus of Spartacus.

Acknowledgments

These poems, written between 2010 and 2013, owe much—in different and sometimes unexpected ways—to Maura Dooley, George Szirtes, Sam Riviere, Tim Cockburn, Katharine Kilalea, Federico Del Vecchio, Gintaras Didžiapetris, Ryan Spring Dooley, Pennacchio Argentato, all at the Palazzo dello Spagnuolo, Nathan Hamilton, Amy Botfield, Caroline Blinder, the Collins family, my grandparents, my aunt, my mother, father, and brothers; and to Hannah Collins, especially.